comix

ARF AND THE METAL DETECTOR

Philip Wooderson

Illustrated by Bridget MacKeith

Hi! I'm Arf. It's amazing what you can find with a metal detector...

A & C Black • London

comix

Published 2001 by A & C Black (Publishers) Ltd
37 Soho Square, London, W1D 3QZ

Text copyright © 2001 Philip Wooderson
Illustrations copyright © 2001 Bridget MacKeith

The rights of Philip Wooderson and Bridget MacKeith to be identified
as author and illustrator of this work have been asserted by them in
accordance with the Copyrights, Designs and Patents Act 1988.

ISBN 0-7136-5914-9

A CIP catalogue for this book is available from the
British Library.

Printed and bound in Spain by G. Z. Printek, Bilbao

CHAPTER ONE

Arf came home from school to find a big box in the hallway.

Hey, Mum, what's this package?

It's not yours.

Gloria was Arf's elder sister.

And Mum won't be back from work for at least another hour.

Arf liked Bill Bott a lot. And Bill Bott got on with Arf.

But what d'you think he's got in here?

It was long and narrow.
The writing on the side said —

Mr. Bill Bott
мм мммм м
мм мммм м

MD 2500 (rechargeable battery included.)

?

When Arf shook the carton, it rattled.

The cardboard flap on the top end was sealed by a short bit of tape — until Arf peeled it off. He had a quick peep inside.

Whatever it is – it's all wrapped up.

Arf managed to push his hand inside and pulled out a little booklet. He opened this on the first page.

WOW!

HOW TO GET THE BEST USE FROM YOUR METAL DETECTOR

Arf couldn't help it. He needed to see what it looked like. Standing on a chair and tilting the box on one end, he joggled it out of the carton.

Unwrapping it wasn't so easy...

Arf saw a red button marked ON/OFF.

He couldn't help pressing the button. A light went on. The machine hummed softly. Holding it in both hands, Arf started to move it about. It bleeped at Mum's umbrella.

hum hum

Too late. Gloria poked her head out from the living room door.

9

Gloria gave him a cruel smile.

I bet you a week's pocket money.

Arf took a very deep breath. He needed his pocket money, because he was saving up to buy a computer game but...

Just give me ten minutes, okay?

CHAPTER TWO

Arf wasn't going to let Gloria have the last laugh about this.

If she wants buried treasure, why shouldn't I find it for her?

Going up to his bedroom Arf picked up a black metal box in which he kept pocket money.

He'd saved £3.21.

It wasn't enough to be treasure, so he went into his mum's room still carrying his money-box.

As he came out of Mum's room, he saw his other sister, Bee. Their pet dog, Hoppa, was waiting there with her.

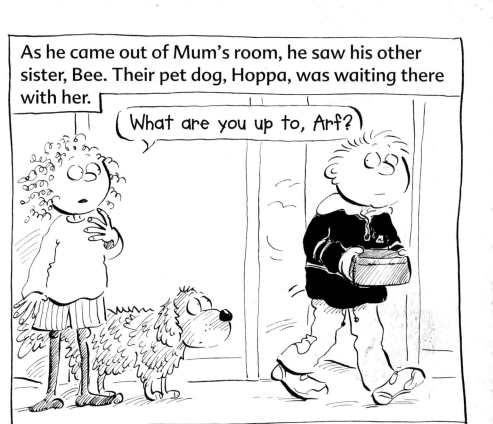

What are you up to, Arf?

Arf decided to ask her to help.

If you're taking Hoppa for his walk, you'll go to the park won't you, Bee?

Why?

16

Arf had to tell her — about the metal detector, and his bet with Gloria.

In that case, you'd better win.

Bee went back to her bedroom and came out a moment later folding a sheet of paper.

I've drawn a plan with a cross on — to show where I'll bury the box.

That's cheating!

The whole thing's cheating!

CHAPTER THREE

Arf waited another ten minutes.

I'm ready to go to the park now!

Gloria followed. She said she was only coming to make sure he would keep out of trouble.

What trouble?

They reached the drinking fountain. Arf couldn't see Bee or Hoppa.

He switched on the metal detector and made for the nearest flowerbed.

Can't you read what it says on that sign over there?

There's nobody here to see me.

DO NOT TREAD ON THE FLOWERBEDS — PENALTY £50

I'm here. I might have to report you!

Not if I find some treasure.

Ha!

Ten minutes went by, without one single bleep.

Arf started to feel a bit worried.

This metal detector's useless. It only works indoors.

It's working outdoors now, stupid. It's telling you THERE'S NO TREASURE!

Another ten minutes went by. Gloria paced up and down.

Mum will be home from work soon.

She'll want to know what you've been up to.

Now Arf was getting desperate. He turned his back on Gloria and pulled Bee's plan from his pocket.

Emergency!

The X on Bee's plan was clearly marked. It was by the third tree on the left.

Striding across, Arf set to work, sweeping the metal detector left and right, back and forth.

He carried on, moving further away from the tree. So much for Bee's plan, he thought crossly. I'll never trust her again. Then —

Nothing so far.

B-e-e-e-e-P

25

None of Mum's beads and bangles was in the metal box. Nor was his £3.21.

It's not my money-box!

Arf couldn't take the wrong box home. But he couldn't go home empty-handed and leave his mum's bedside drawer empty.

Perhaps I could borrow a few of these things?

Taking a handful of jewellery, Arf re-buried the box.

CHAPTER FOUR

Back home, he shoved the jewellery into Mum's bedside drawer, hoping she wouldn't look closely and notice her beads had gone missing.

Her stuff didn't look that much better.

But where had her stuff disappeared to? Arf needed to talk to Bee. She was now back from her walk.

You've been playing some trick on me, Bee.

Sorry?

She didn't look sorry. But when Arf told her about finding that box full of jewellery, she did look very puzzled.

Arf felt even more confused. But Mum might be home any moment. He needed to concentrate on packing the metal detector back in its cardboard carton.

Why won't this flap stay shut?

He had to seal it with parcel tape out of the kitchen cupboard. He was still trying to cut the tape when he heard a key in the lock.

He jumped back as the front door opened.

Hello, Mum. Only looking.

Mum looked at the tape and the scissors, then the label on the package.

But this is for Mr Bott.

So?

So what were you up to, Arf?

He was saved by a knock on the door.

That's Bill Bott, Mum!

Hello, hello!

Mum wasn't too keen on talking to Bill, not after a hard day's work. She thought he was a boring old boffer.

I'm tired. I'm going upstairs. I'll leave you to handle this, Arf.

33

Bill Bott got down on his knees and struggled to open the carton.

You want to come out for a trial run?

Out in the park?

Great idea, yes!
We might even find buried treasure —
if I can undo all this tape!
What kind of clumsy fool
wrapped it up like this?

Perhaps
he was
just in a hurry?

Gloria gave Arf a nasty nudge.

Arf!

34

39

Mr Bott sucked his cheeks in.

CHAPTER FIVE

Next morning Arf and Bill Bott turned up outside the park as the keeper was opening the gates.

Arf led the way to the fountain. Then Bill put down his bag and Arf got out Bee's plan.

Bill studied the plan for some time, turning it round and round.

Your money-box is by the third tree on the left, south of the drinking fountain.

But as Arf went to get the trowel a police car roared down the avenue and squealed to a halt near Bill.

Three policemen piled out. They hurried across to the flowerbed.

Arf waited and watched, horrified, as they surrounded Bill and took the metal detector. They seemed to be asking Bill questions.

Bill kept shaking his head. But they made him get in their car and they drove off with a screeching of tyres.

Oh corrr – that's amazing.

Arf grinned with delight. Then another thought crossed his mind.

You don't think they buried their loot in that box – the one I found in the park?

I do.

So poor Mr Bott has been caught digging up stolen goods. He'll have some explaining to do.

Arf's jaw dropped.

He was only helping me!

The police don't know that, Arf. And you got him into this mess.

But before Mum could phone the police and tell them what Arf had been up to, the front door bell chimed.

DRRIINNG

It was Bill!

48

CHAPTER SIX

Mum was wringing her hands.

Oh Bill – Arf is terribly sorry!

Oh no, please forget it. I've had an incredible time!

He was grinning and flushed with excitement.

The police had a tip-off about some jewellery thieves. I was able to tell them exactly where to look. Thanks to Bee and my metal detector!

Two boxes in the same place? NO.

So had Bee made a mistake with her plan? Or had he made a mistake? He remembered Bill turning the plan round and round.

Your money-box is by the third tree on the left, south of the drinking fountain.

Arf hadn't checked that the first time, thanks to Gloria breathing down his neck! Supposing he'd read it the wrong way up?

I NEED to go to the park, Mum!

I've got something to tell the police.

In the park, Arf ran down the avenue towards the drinking fountain, with Bill Bott puffing behind him.

Arf shook his head.

No, you've blown it...

Unless —

When those thieves robbed the jewellers – did they really pretend they were workmen changing the jewellers' shop window?

We haven't got time to go into that now.

Why not? It might be CRUCIAL!

Like – how?

58

59

CHAPTER SEVEN

The 'workmen' did not hang about...

...but neither did the policemen.

When the gang had been bundled into a van and driven away at top speed, Arf turned and noticed Hoppa hard at work in the flowerbed.

But when the local paper came out, Mum showed them all the front page.